The MAILBOX®
The Education Center®

For Every Learner™
Math

grade 2

3 Differentiated Activities for Every Skill

- Two-digit addition
- Two-digit subtraction
- Place value
- Comparing numbers
- Ordering numbers

- Word problems
- Fractions
- Geometry
- Time
- Money

Covers 18 key skills!

Written by Laura Mihalenko

Managing Editor: Kelly Robertson

Editorial Team: Becky S. Andrews, Diane Badden, Kimberley Bruck, Karen A. Brudnak, Kitty Campbell, Chris Curry, Lynette Dickerson, Theresa Lewis Goode, Tazmen Hansen, Marsha Heim, Lori Z. Henry, Angela Kamstra-Jacobson, Debra Liverman, Dorothy C. McKinney, Thad H. McLaurin, Sharon Murphy, Jennifer Nunn, Gerri Primak, Mark Rainey, Greg D. Rieves, Hope Rodgers, Rebecca Saunders, Barry Slate, Zane Williard

www.themailbox.com

©2009 The Mailbox® Books
All rights reserved.
ISBN10 #1-56234-874-4 • ISBN13 #978-156234-874-8

Manufactured in the United States
10 9 8 7 6 5 4 3 2 1

Table of Contents

Practice each skill **3** different ways!

What's Inside

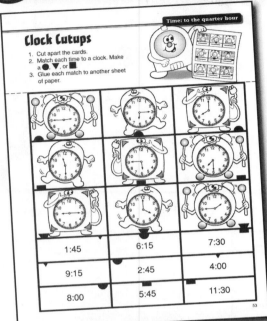

Clock Cutups

Time: to the quarter hour

1. Cut apart the cards.
2. Match each time to a clock. Make a ●, ▼, or ■.
3. Glue each match to another sheet of paper.

1:45	6:15	7:30
9:15	2:45	4:00
8:00	5:45	11:30

A Busy Day

Time: to the quarter hour

(Pages 55 and 56)

1. Write the time on each card.
2. Cut apart the cards.
3. Order the cards from the earliest time to the latest time.
4. On your other page, glue the cards in order.

Formats and levels of difficulty vary!

A Busy Day

Time: to the quarter hour

Name

1. Wake up. — 7:00 AM
2. Eat breakfast.
3. Get dressed.
4. Go to school.
5. Eat lunch.
6. Come home.
7. Eat a snack. — 4:15 PM
8. Play outside. — 5:00 PM
9. Do homework.
10. Eat dinner.
11. Read a book.
12. Go to bed. — 8:30 PM

Time to Measure

Time: to the quarter hour

Name

Write the time shown on each clock.
Color the spice jar with the matching time.

A. ___ B. ___ C. ___ D. ___

E. ___ F. ___

Pssst! There are two extra spice jars.

Kiss the Cook

9:45 3:30 5:30
10:15 11:15 6:00 8:30 1:45 2:00 4:45 12:15
7:45

G. ___ H. ___ I. ___ J. ___

Skills Checklist

Assessment Code
M = More practice needed
S = Successful

Skills	Practice 1	Practice 2	Practice 3	Notes
Addition: no regrouping				
Subtraction: no regrouping				
Addition: with regrouping				
Subtraction: with regrouping				
Place value: to 1,000				
Comparing numbers: to 1,000				
Ordering numbers: to 1,000				
Word problems: choose an operation				
Word problems: adding or subtracting money				
Fractions: comparing				
Plane shapes				
Solid figures				
Time: to the quarter hour				
Money: coin values				
Organizing data				
Interpreting data				
Number patterns				
Algebraic thinking: addition and subtraction				

Note to the teacher: To track the skill progress of individual students, personalize copies of the page. Each time a student completes a practice page, use the provided code to note an assessment of his work.

Tie-Dyed Turtle

Add.
Color the section of the turtle shell with the matching answer.

A. $\begin{array}{r} 43 \\ + 13 \\ \hline 56 \end{array}$

B. $\begin{array}{r} 51 \\ + 22 \\ \hline \end{array}$

C. $\begin{array}{r} 32 \\ + 11 \\ \hline \end{array}$

D. $\begin{array}{r} 75 \\ + 20 \\ \hline \end{array}$

E. $\begin{array}{r} 18 \\ + 41 \\ \hline \end{array}$

F. $\begin{array}{r} 60 \\ + 24 \\ \hline \end{array}$

G. $\begin{array}{r} 84 \\ + 13 \\ \hline \end{array}$

H. $\begin{array}{r} 26 \\ + 23 \\ \hline \end{array}$

I. $\begin{array}{r} 35 \\ + 31 \\ \hline \end{array}$

J. $\begin{array}{r} 41 \\ + 34 \\ \hline \end{array}$

K. $\begin{array}{r} 67 \\ + 10 \\ \hline \end{array}$

L. $\begin{array}{r} 24 \\ + 64 \\ \hline \end{array}$

Something Fishy

(Pages 6 and 7)

1. Cut apart the cards.
2. Match the pairs of fish.
3. Write each pair of numbers as an addition problem next to the matching letter on your other page.
4. Solve each problem.

For Every Learner™: Math • ©The Mailbox® Books • TEC61196

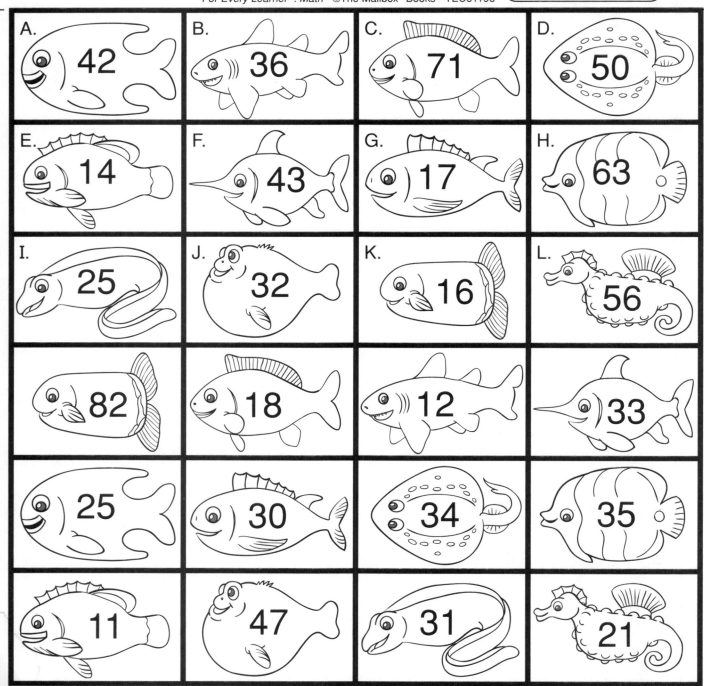

A. 42
B. 36
C. 71
D. 50
E. 14
F. 43
G. 17
H. 63
I. 25
J. 32
K. 16
L. 56
82
18
12
33
25
30
34
35
11
47
31
21

Something Fishy

A.   B.   C.   D.   E.

$+$ $+$ $+$ $+$ $+$

F.   G.   H.   I.   J.

$+$ $+$ $+$ $+$ $+$

K.   L.

$+$ $+$

Be back soon!

For Every Learner™: Math • ©The Mailbox® Books • TEC61196 • Key p. 77

Note to the teacher: Use with "Something Fishy" on page 6.

7

Start Your Engines!

1. Cut out the wheels below.
2. Use a brad to attach each wheel to the racecar so that "Start" is showing.
3. Starting with Wheel A, turn the wheel one space. Write the problem on another sheet of paper and solve it.
4. Repeat Step 3 with each space on Wheel A.
5. Then repeat Step 3 for each space on Wheel B.

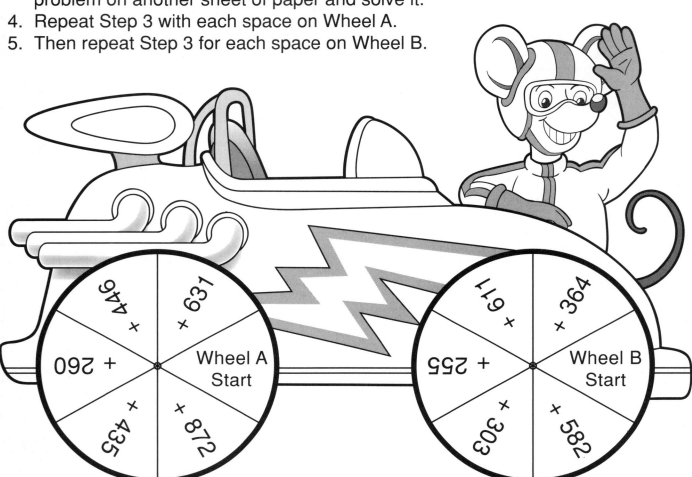

Wheel A
Start

+ 446
+ 631
+ 260
+ 435
+ 872

Wheel B
Start

+ 611
+ 364
+ 255
+ 303
+ 582

For Every Learner™: Math • ©The Mailbox® Books • TEC61196 • Key p. 77

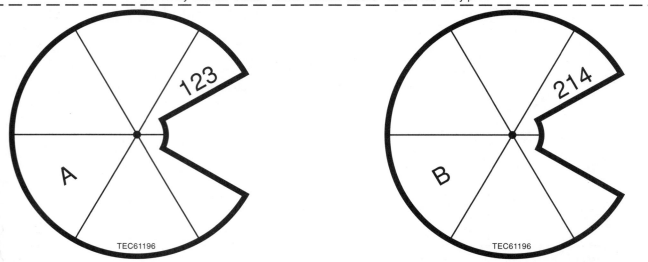

123

A

TEC61196

214

B

TEC61196

A Toothy Grin

Subtract.
Cut out the triangles.
Put a dot of glue on each •.
Glue each triangle to its matching tooth.

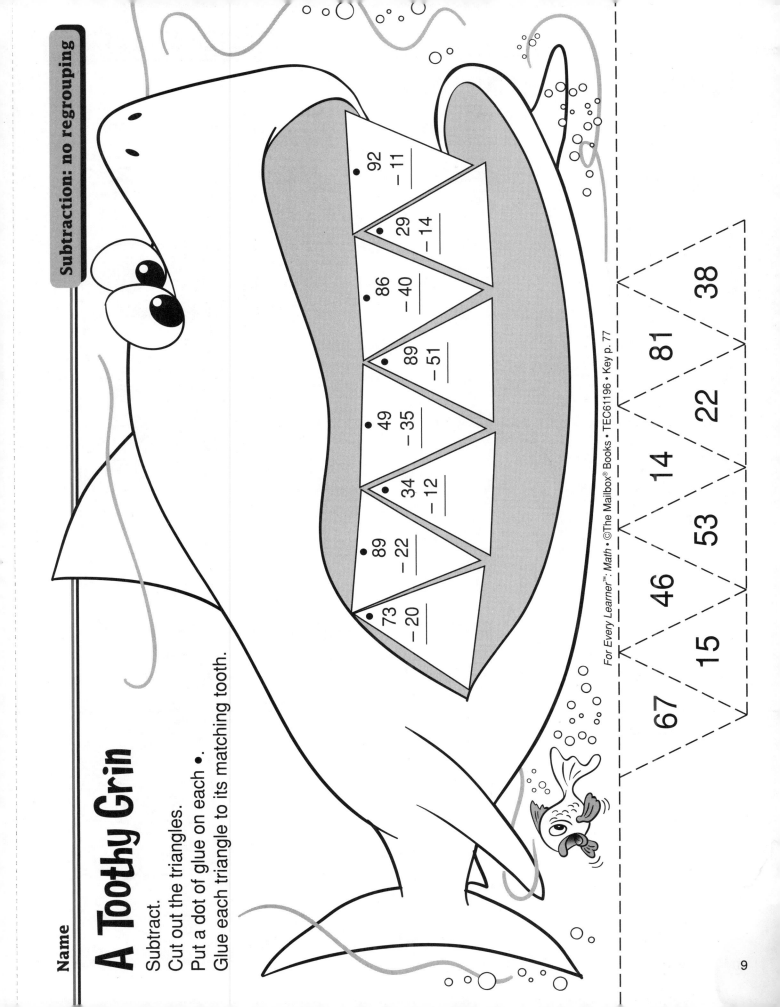

92	29	86	89	49	34	89	73
−11	−14	−40	−51	−35	−12	−22	−20

| 67 | 15 | 46 | 53 | 14 | 22 | 81 | 38 |

Which Mouse?

Use the two numbers on each computer mouse to write a subtraction problem. Solve each problem.

A.   57   12

B.   67   44

C.   74   24

D.   83   31

E.   95   32

F.   41   20

G.   59   15

H.   78   35

I.   56   12

J.   49   26

My mouse has a difference of 63!

Color the cat's mouse.

For Every Learner™: Math • ©The Mailbox® Books • TEC61196 • Key p. 77

Stargazing

(Pages 11 and 12)

1. Cut apart the cards. Stack the star and moon cards in separate piles.
2. Choose one card from each pile.
3. Use the numbers on the cards to write a subtraction problem on your other page.
4. Solve each problem.

For Every Learner™: Math • ©The Mailbox® Books • TEC61196

103	214	332	420
341	142	230	545
413	234	105	532
556	668	686	799
766	887	879	997
978	986	787	598

Stargazing

A. ___

B. ___

C. ___

D. ___

E. ___

F. ___

G. ___

H. ___

I. ___

J. ___

K. ___

L. ___

Was the number on the star card or the moon card first in each problem? Explain why.

_____

_____

_____

For Every Learner™: *Math* • ©The Mailbox® Books • TEC61196

Note to the teacher: Use with "Stargazing" on page 11.

Barnyard Baking

Add.

A.
$$\begin{array}{r} {\scriptstyle 1} \\ 68 \\ + 12 \\ \hline 80 \end{array}$$

B.
$$\begin{array}{r} {\scriptstyle 1} \\ 35 \\ + 16 \\ \hline 1 \end{array}$$

C.
$$\begin{array}{r} {\scriptstyle 1} \\ 27 \\ + 19 \\ \hline 6 \end{array}$$

E.
$$\begin{array}{r} {\scriptstyle 1} \\ 39 \\ + 29 \\ \hline 8 \end{array}$$

F.
$$\begin{array}{r} 49 \\ + 18 \\ \hline \end{array}$$

H.
$$\begin{array}{r} 24 \\ + 58 \\ \hline \end{array}$$

M.
$$\begin{array}{r} 75 \\ + 18 \\ \hline \end{array}$$

S.
$$\begin{array}{r} 37 \\ + 36 \\ \hline \end{array}$$

How do chickens make cakes?

To solve the riddle, write each letter from above on
its matching numbered line or lines below.

T __ __ Y   __ __ K __   __ R O __   __ __ R __ T __ __ !
  82 68   51 80 68   67   93   73 46   80   46 82

A Perfect Fit
(Pages 14 and 15)

1. Cut apart the cards below.
2. Match the shapes on the cards to the problems on your other page.
3. Write and solve each addition problem.

For Every Learner™: Math • ©The Mailbox® Books • TEC61196

25	39
46	54
66	28
37	15

A Perfect Fit

A.
1
28
+ 25
—————
53

B.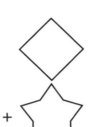
+ _____

C.
+ _____

D.
+ _____

E.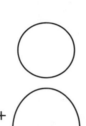
+ _____

F.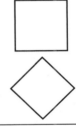
+ _____

G.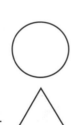
+ _____

H.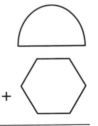
+ _____

I.
+ _____

J.

+ _____

For Every Learner™: Math • ©The Mailbox® Books • TEC61196 • Key p. 77

Note to the teacher: Use with "A Perfect Fit" on page 14.

Here's the Scoop

1. Cut apart the cards.
2. Divide a large sheet of paper into two columns and label one column "Correct" and the other column "Incorrect."
3. Check the answer to the problem on each card.
4. Glue each card in the matching column.

For Every Learner™: Math • ©The Mailbox® Books • TEC61196 • Key p. 77

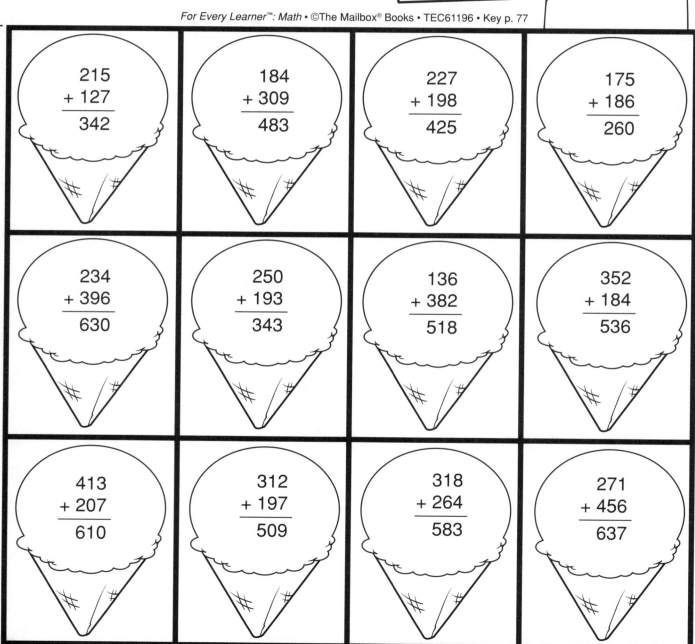

215
+ 127
342

184
+ 309
483

227
+ 198
425

175
+ 186
260

234
+ 396
630

250
+ 193
343

136
+ 382
518

352
+ 184
536

413
+ 207
610

312
+ 197
509

318
+ 264
583

271
+ 456
637

Get in the Game

Directions for two players:

1. Put your game markers on START.
2. In turn, spin the spinner and move your marker. (If your spin has you move back on your first turn, your turn is over.)
3. Solve the problem on scrap paper and say your answer.
4. If correct, leave your marker. If incorrect, move your marker back one space.
5. The first player to reach FINISH wins.

START

FINISH

$$53 - 38$$

$$80 - 24$$

$$42 - 15$$

Move back 1 space.

Move ahead 2 spaces.

Move ahead 1 space.

Move back 1 space.

$$60 - 16$$

$$80 - 27$$

Move ahead 2 spaces.

Lose a turn.

Move back 1 space.

Move ahead 2 spaces.

$$85 - 47$$

$$92 - 68$$

$$60 - 28$$

$$82 - 29$$

$$61 - 12$$

Keeping the Beat

Subtract.
Cross out the matching difference on the drum.

A.
$$\begin{array}{r} \overset{3}{4}\overset{1}{0} \\ -14 \\ \hline 26 \end{array}$$

B.
$$\begin{array}{r} 32 \\ -19 \\ \hline \end{array}$$

C.
$$\begin{array}{r} 81 \\ -25 \\ \hline \end{array}$$

D.
$$\begin{array}{r} 42 \\ -34 \\ \hline \end{array}$$

E.
$$\begin{array}{r} 95 \\ -37 \\ \hline \end{array}$$

F.
$$\begin{array}{r} 62 \\ -46 \\ \hline \end{array}$$

G.
$$\begin{array}{r} 77 \\ -48 \\ \hline \end{array}$$

H.
$$\begin{array}{r} 61 \\ -52 \\ \hline \end{array}$$

I.
$$\begin{array}{r} 70 \\ -53 \\ \hline \end{array}$$

J.
$$\begin{array}{r} 83 \\ -67 \\ \hline \end{array}$$

K.
$$\begin{array}{r} 96 \\ -77 \\ \hline \end{array}$$

L.
$$\begin{array}{r} 90 \\ -65 \\ \hline \end{array}$$

A Stylin' Lion

(Pages 19 and 20)

1. Cut apart the cards and sort each set of three cards into separate piles.
2. Use each set of cards to write three subtraction problems in the matching row on your other page.
3. Solve each problem.

For Every Learner™: Math • ©The Mailbox® Books • TEC61196

561	607	254
247	456	739
962	571	128
740	321	806
658	364	129

TEC61196

A Stylin' Lion

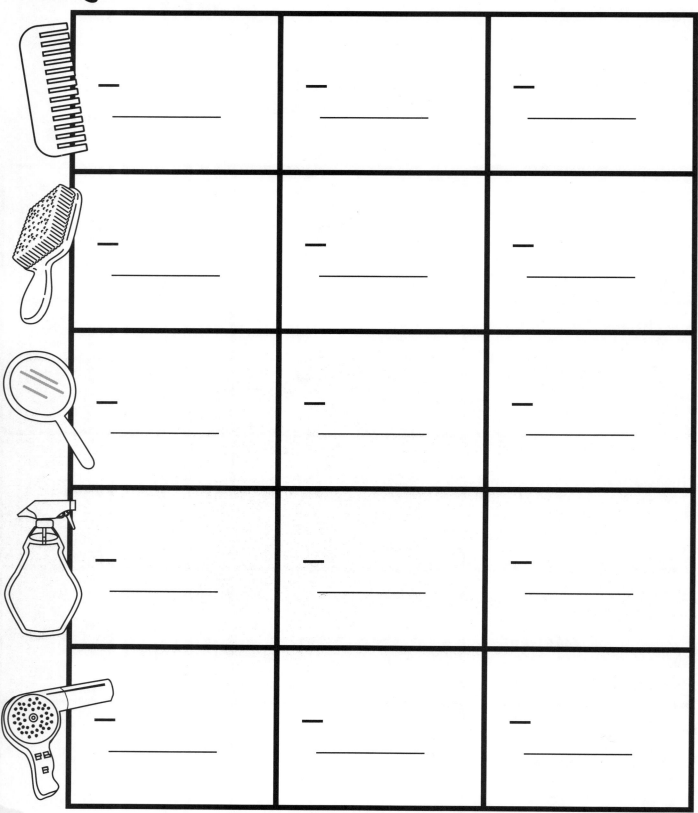

Note to the teacher: Use with "A Stylin' Lion" on page 19.

The Early Bird

Write each number.
Cut apart the boxes and glue each one over
its matching answer.

1 hundred 4 tens 6 ones

3 hundreds 0 tens 5 ones

6 hundreds 1 ten 3 ones

4 hundreds 9 tens 0 ones

5 hundreds 3 tens 6 ones

9 hundreds 7 tens 4 ones

7 hundreds 2 tens 1 one

8 hundreds 5 tens 7 ones

1 thousand 0 hundreds 0 tens 0 ones

3 hundreds 8 tens 9 ones

4 hundreds 0 tens 8 ones

7 hundreds 6 tens 0 ones

146

389	146	490	721	613	760
536	974	408	305	1,000	857

Down the Mountain

(Pages 22 and 23)

1. Cut apart the cards below.
2. On your other page, write the number represented on each card in the two different ways as shown.

For Every Learner™: Math • ©The Mailbox® Books • TEC61196

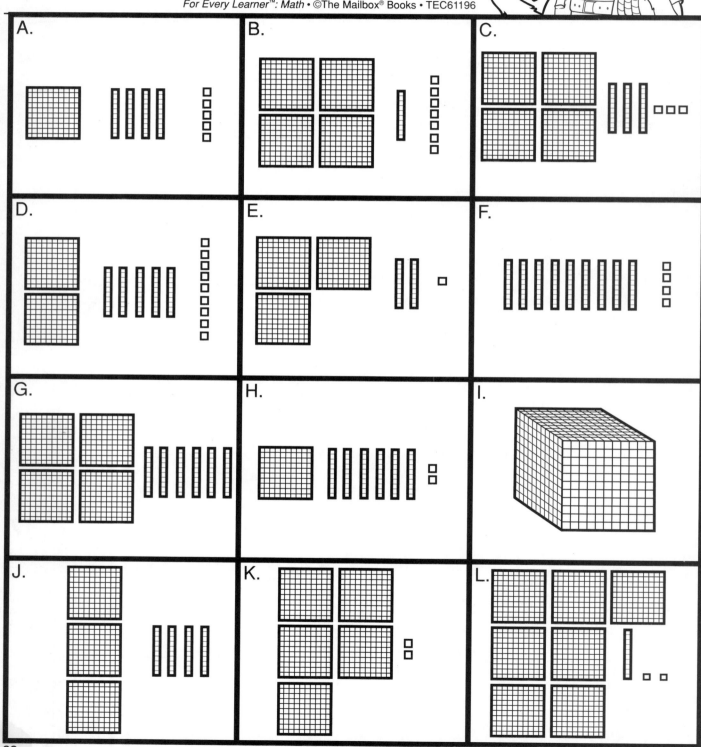

Down the Mountain

	Number	Value of Each Digit
A.	145	1 hundred 4 tens 5 ones
B.		
C.		
D.		
E.		
F.		
G.		
H.		
I.		
J.		
K.		
L.		

For Every Learner™: Math • ©The Mailbox® Books • TEC61196 • Key p. 77

Note to the teacher: Use with "Down the Mountain" on page 22.

23

Snail Mail

Write the value of the underlined digit on each envelope's stamp.
Then use the color code to trace each envelope.

Color Code

ones = blue
tens = red
hundreds = green
thousands = yellow

Why is the zero
needed in 704 if zero
tens equal zero?

_____
_____
_____
_____
_____

1̲26 □	2̲36̲ □	1̲63 □
704 □	407̲ □	795̲ □
8̲61 □	3̲67̲ □	692̲ □
2̲72̲ □	1̲,000 □	9̲58̲ □
530̲ □	349̲ □	518̲ □

For Every Learner™: *Math* • ©The Mailbox® Books • TEC61196 • Key p. 78

Bobbing for Apples

1. Cut out the puzzle pieces.
2. Use the pieces with true number sentences to put together the puzzle.
3. Glue the puzzle pieces on the tub.

For Every Learner™: Math • ©The Mailbox® Books • TEC61196 • Key p. 78

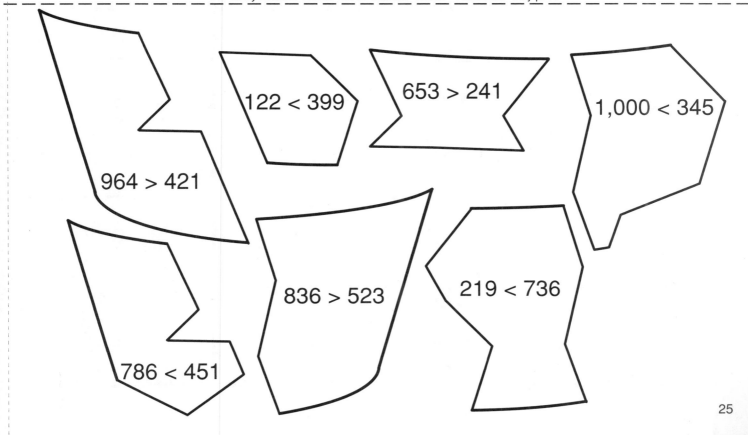

964 > 421

122 < 399

653 > 241

1,000 < 345

786 < 451

836 > 523

219 < 736

All the Buzz!

(Pages 26 and 27)

1. Cut apart the cards below and place them facedown.

2. Choose two cards. Compare the numbers and write them in the spaces by letter A on your other page to make a true number sentence.

3. Return the cards facedown and repeat Step 2 for each section of the beehive.

For Every Learner™: *Math* • ©The Mailbox® Books • TEC61196

153	207	391	1,000
515	623	714	882
279	356	408	139

Name

All the Buzz!

A. _____ > _____

B. _____ < _____

C. _____ > _____

D. _____ < _____

E. _____ > _____

F. _____ < _____

G. _____ > _____

H. _____ < _____

I. _____ > _____

J. _____ < _____

K. _____ > _____

L. _____ < _____

For Every Learner™: Math • ©The Mailbox® Books • TEC61196

Note to the teacher: Use with "All the Buzz!" on page 27.

27

Prizeworthy Pups

Write >, <, or =.

A. 317 ◯ 337

B. 691 ◯ 619

C. 791 ◯ 793

D. 1,000 ◯ 988

E. 127 ◯ 127

F. 909 ◯ 809

G. 454 ◯ 456

H. 930 ◯ 930

I. 281 ◯ 280

J. 344 ◯ 433

K. 499 ◯ 501

L. 556 ◯ 656

M. 284 ◯ 289

N. 895 ◯ 895

O. 1,000 ◯ 999

Best in Class

291 < 2 ___1
Is there a number that
can make this number
sentence true? _____

Explain._____

_____

_____

Stringing Beads

(Pages 29 and 30)

1. Cut apart the cards.
2. Sort the cards by letter.
3. Glue each set of cards in order from smallest to largest on your other page.

For Every Learner™: Math • ©The Mailbox® Books • TEC61196

A. **999**	A. **1,000**	A. **998**	A. **997**
B. **318**	B. **319**	B. **315**	B. **316**
C. **801**	C. **798**	C. **802**	C. **800**
D. **461**	D. **459**	D. **460**	D. **463**
E. **530**	E. **531**	E. **529**	E. **532**
F. **678**	F. **675**	F. **677**	F. **676**

Stringing Beads

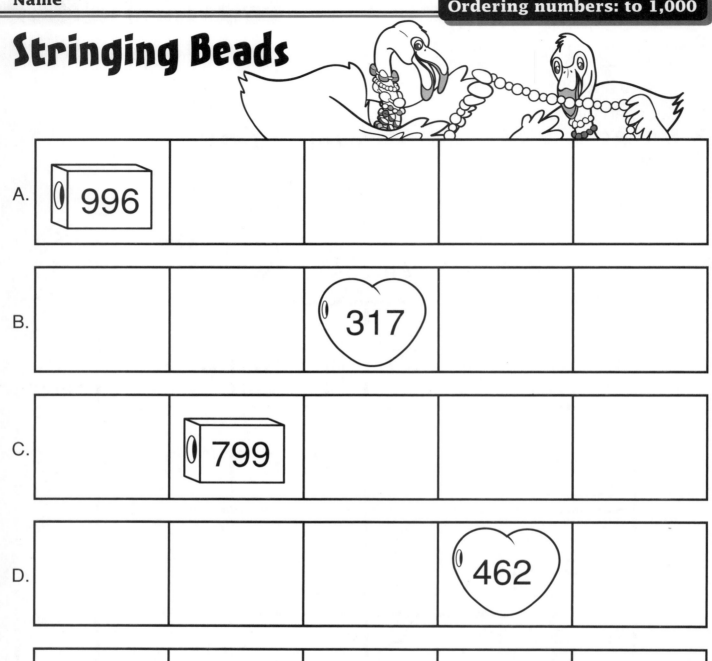

A. | 996 | | | |

B. | | | 317 | | |

C. | | 799 | | | |

D. | | | | 462 | |

E. | 528 | | | | |

F. | | | | | 679 |

Note to the teacher: Use with "Stringing Beads" on page 29.

Growing in the Garden

1. Cut apart the cards.
2. Sort the cards by flower.
3. Glue each set of cards in order from smallest to largest on another sheet of paper.

For Every Learner™: *Math* • ©The Mailbox® Books • TEC61196 • Key p. 78

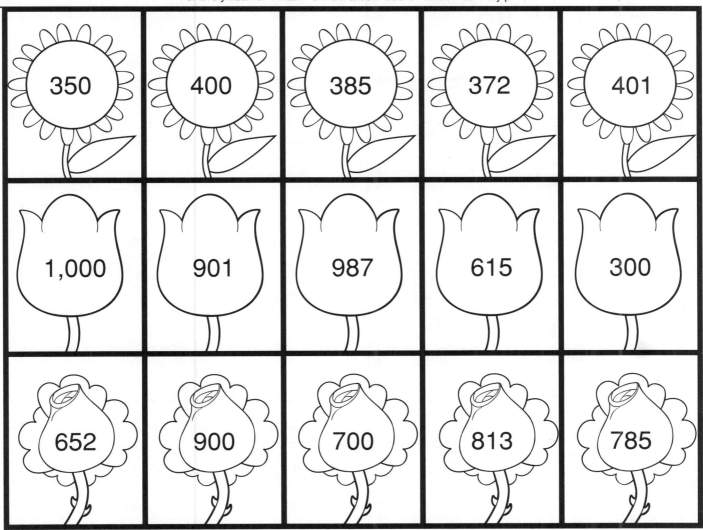

350	400	385	372	401
1,000	901	987	615	300
652	900	700	813	785

32

Name _____

Gone Fishing

Use the numbers on each fish to write six different three-digit numbers on the bubbles.
Then write the numbers in each set in the order shown.

greatest to least

_____, _____, _____, _____, _____, _____

greatest to least

_____, _____, _____, _____, _____, _____

Write the largest number from each set and the number 1,000 in order from greatest to least.

_____, _____, _____

least to greatest

_____, _____, _____, _____, _____, _____

least to greatest

_____, _____, _____, _____, _____, _____

least to greatest

_____, _____, _____, _____, _____, _____

For Every Learner™: Math • ©The Mailbox® Books • TEC61196 • Key p. 78

Bella's Buttons

(Pages 33 and 34)

1. Cut apart the cards below.
2. Use the cards to help you write and solve a number sentence for each problem on your other page.
3. Color the button with the matching answer on your other page.

For Every Learner™: Math • ©The Mailbox® Books • TEC61196

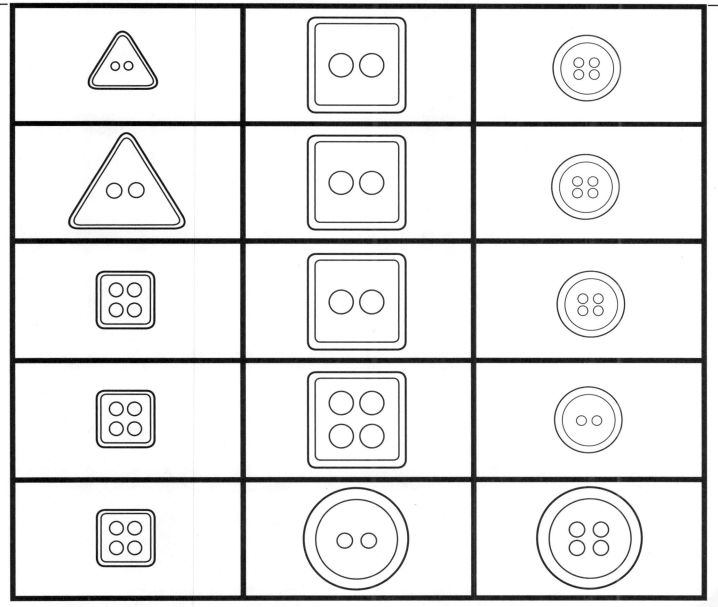

Bella's Buttons

A. Bella has 7 large buttons and 8 small buttons. How many buttons does she have **in all?**

$$7 + 8 = 15 \text{ buttons}$$

B. Bella takes out her 8 small buttons. She puts away the buttons that only have two holes. How many small buttons does she have **left?**

C. How many square and circle-shaped buttons does Bella have **altogether?**

D. How many **more** 4-holed buttons than 2-holed buttons does Bella have?

E. Bella gives 6 of her buttons to a friend. How many does she have **left?**

F. How many circle-shaped and triangle-shaped buttons does Bella have **altogether?**

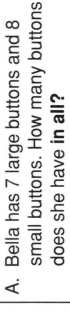

For Every Learner™: Math • ©The Mailbox® Books • TEC61196 • Key p. 78

Note to the teacher: Use with "Bella's Buttons" on page 33.

The Crayon Factory

Read each word problem.
Cut out the matching addition or
    subtraction problem and solve it.
Glue each number sentence in its
    matching box.

A. The crayon factory makes 43 red crayons and 36 blue crayons each day. How many red and blue crayons are made each day in all?	B. There are 78 green crayons and 26 black crayons in a container. How many more green crayons are there than black? 
C. 97 yellow and brown crayons spilled on the factory floor. 42 of the crayons are yellow. How many of the crayons are brown?	D. The purple crayon machine made 47 crayons. Then it made 38 more. How many purple crayons did the machine make in all? 
E. A large crayon box holds 64 crayons. There are 21 crayons in the box. How many more crayons are needed to fill the box? 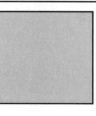	F. A small crayon box holds 24 crayons. How many crayons will two small boxes hold altogether? 

For Every Learner™: Math • ©The Mailbox® Books • TEC61196 • Key p. 78

78 + 26	47 + 38	43 + 36	97 + 42	24 + 24	78 + 26
24 − 2	78 − 26	64 − 21	47 − 38	43 − 36	97 − 42

At the Sweet Shop

1. Write a number sentence for each word problem and solve it.
2. Cut apart the cards.
3. Sort the cards into two sets: one with addition number sentences and one with subtraction number sentences.
4. Divide another sheet of paper into two columns. Label one column "Addition" and the other "Subtraction."
5. Glue each set of cards in the matching column.

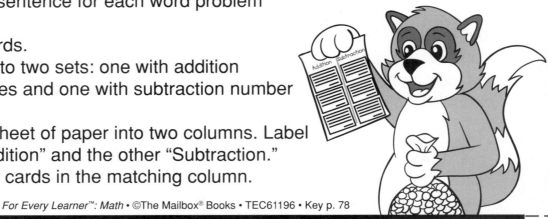

For Every Learner™: Math • ©The Mailbox® Books • TEC61196 • Key p. 78

A. Ricky has 126 jelly beans in his bag. He has 49 more gumdrops than jelly beans. How many gumdrops does he have in all? _____ gumdrops	B. Ricky has 83 peppermints and lollipops in all. He has 35 peppermints. How many lollipops does he have? _____ lollipops
C. Ricky has 126 candies and sticks of gum in all. He has 52 candies. How many sticks of gum does he have? _____ sticks of gum	D. Ricky has 48 lollipops. He has 17 more licorice sticks than lollipops. How many licorice sticks does he have? _____ licorice sticks
E. Ricky has 83 peppermints and 65 licorice sticks. How many more peppermints than licorice sticks does he have? _____ peppermints	F. Ricky has 74 jelly beans and 65 licorice sticks. How many jelly beans and licorice sticks does he have altogether? _____ jelly beans and licorice sticks

In the Bank

1. Cut apart the cards.
2. Solve each problem.
3. Sort the cards into two sets: one with answers greater than $5.00 and one with answers less than $5.00.
4. Glue each set on another sheet of paper and then label each set.

Penny has $1.46 in her bank. She puts $4.42 more in. How much does she have in her bank in all?	Paul has $4.63 in his bank. He takes $2.41 out. How much money does he have left?	Pete's bank has $3.14 in it and Patti's bank has $4.23 in it. How much do the banks have in them altogether?
$ ___.___ + ___.___ ‾‾‾‾‾‾ $ ___.___	$ ___.___ − ___.___ ‾‾‾‾‾‾ $ ___.___	$ ___.___ + ___.___ ‾‾‾‾‾‾ $ ___.___
Pam's bank has $7.96 in it and Peg's bank has $3.24 in it. How much more money does Pam have in her bank than Peg?	Perry puts $1.24 into his bank. Now there is $4.78 in his bank. How much money was in Perry's bank before?	Peggy has $4.12 in her bank. She puts $5.81 more in. How much does she have in her bank now?
$ ___.___ − ___.___ ‾‾‾‾‾‾ $ ___.___	$ ___.___ − ___.___ ‾‾‾‾‾‾ $ ___.___	$ ___.___ + ___.___ ‾‾‾‾‾‾ $ ___.___

Hats For Sale!

(Pages 38 and 39)

1. Cut apart the cards.
2. Use the cards to help you solve the problems on your other page. Make sure to show your work.

cowboy hat	baseball cap	bucket hat

$5.52	$6.78	$2.45

beret	sombrero	stocking cap
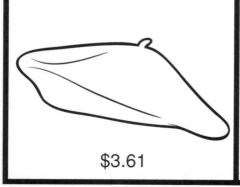		
$3.61	$4.34	$1.20

Hats for Sale!

1. Henry's first customer buys a cowboy hat and a bucket hat. How much do the two hats cost altogether?	2. Another customer buys a beret. She gives Henry $4.75. How much change will she get back?	3. How much more does a baseball cap cost than a sombrero?
4. Henry's next customer buys a stocking cap and a beret. What is the total cost?	5. How much would it cost altogether to buy a stocking cap and a bucket hat?	6. How much more does a cowboy hat cost than a stocking cap?

Note to the teacher: Use with "Hats for Sale!" on page 38.

39

All Around Town

Read each event of Maddie Mouse's day.
Write and solve a problem to show how much money Maddie had after each event.

Maddie left her house with $6.85.

1. She paid a $0.72 fine
   at the library.

2. When she left the library,
   Maddie found $1.84
   on the sidewalk.

3. She stopped at the
   candy store and spent $2.11.

4. Maddie dropped three
   quarters when she left
   the candy store.

5. When Maddie got home,
   she did her chores and
   received $2.75 for her
   allowance.

6. How much more money
   did Maddie have at the end
   of the day than when she left
   the house?

Tiger's Fix-It Shop

1. Color each shape to show the fraction.
2. Cut apart the cards.
3. Sort the cards into two sets: more than $\frac{1}{2}$ and less than $\frac{1}{2}$.
4. Glue and label each set on another sheet of paper.

For Every Learner™: Math • ©The Mailbox® Books • TEC61196 • Key p. 78

$\frac{2}{3}$	$\frac{1}{4}$	$\frac{2}{5}$
$\frac{3}{4}$	$\frac{6}{8}$	$\frac{1}{3}$
$\frac{1}{6}$	$\frac{5}{6}$	$\frac{3}{5}$
$\frac{4}{6}$	$\frac{2}{8}$	$\frac{1}{5}$

A Hole in One

(Pages 42 and 43)

Directions for two players:

1. Cut apart the cards and stack them facedown.
2. Place your game markers on Start.
3. In turn, draw a card and compare the fraction on the card to the one on your gameboard space. Then tell which fraction is larger or whether the two fractions are equal.
4. If correct, roll a die and move your marker. If incorrect, your turn is over.
5. The first player to reach Finish wins.

For Every Learner™: Math • ©The Mailbox® Books • TEC61196

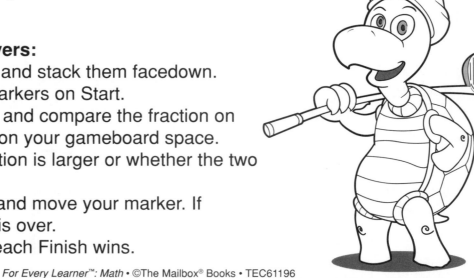

A Hole in One

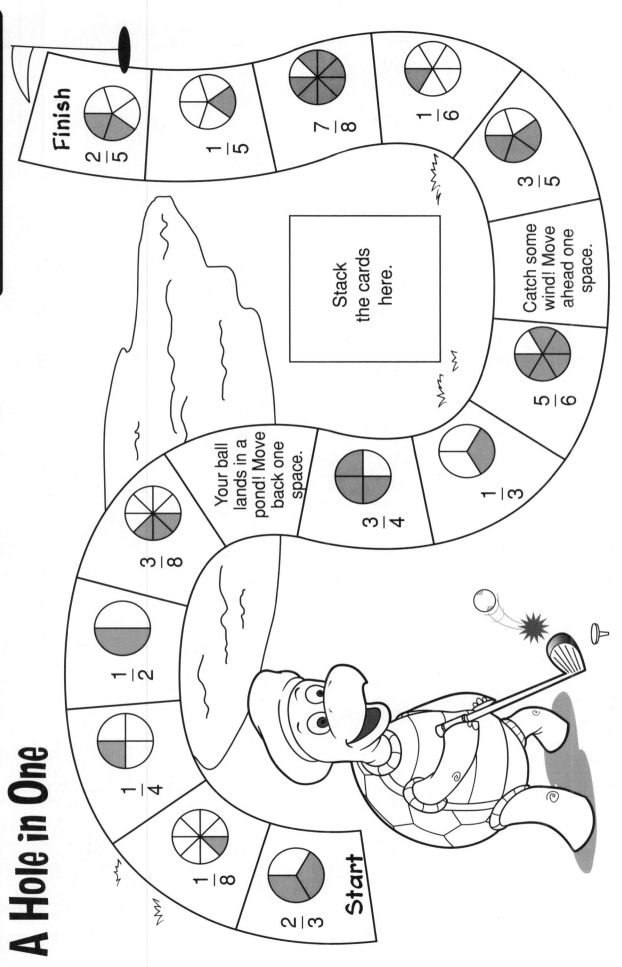

Note to the teacher: Use with "A Hole in One" on page 42.

For Every Learner™: Math • ©The Mailbox® Books • TEC61196

Perfect Pies!

Color each circle to show the fraction.
Write >, <, or = in each ☐.

A.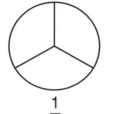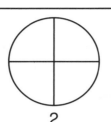

$\frac{1}{3}$ ☐ $\frac{2}{4}$

B.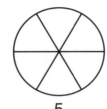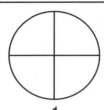

$\frac{5}{6}$ ☐ $\frac{1}{4}$

C.

$\frac{2}{5}$ ☐ $\frac{2}{3}$

D.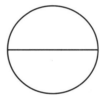

$\frac{3}{6}$ ☐ $\frac{1}{2}$

E.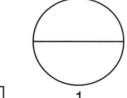

$\frac{4}{8}$ ☐ $\frac{1}{2}$

F.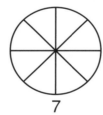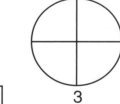

$\frac{7}{8}$ ☐ $\frac{3}{4}$

G.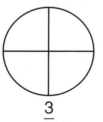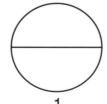

$\frac{3}{4}$ ☐ $\frac{2}{3}$

H.

$\frac{1}{2}$ ☐ $\frac{4}{5}$

I.

$\frac{1}{8}$ ☐ $\frac{1}{4}$

J.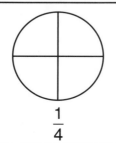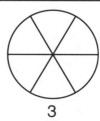

$\frac{2}{3}$ ☐ $\frac{3}{6}$

For Every Learner™: Math • ©The Mailbox® Books • TEC61196 • Key p. 79

Shaping Up
(Pages 45 and 46)

1. Cut out the puzzle pieces below.
2. Glue each puzzle piece to the matching description on your other page.

For Every Learner™: Math • ©The Mailbox® Books • TEC61196

circle

square

rectangle

triangle

hexagon

pentagon

Shaping Up

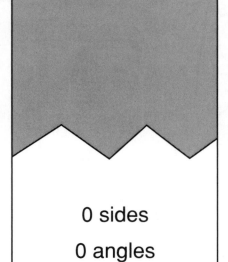

3 sides

3 angles

0 sides

0 angles

4 sides

4 angles

All sides are of equal length.

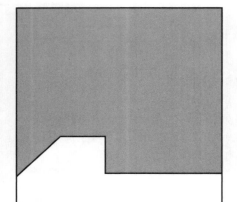

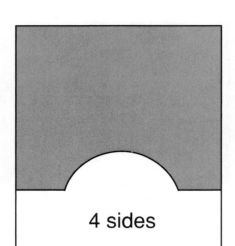

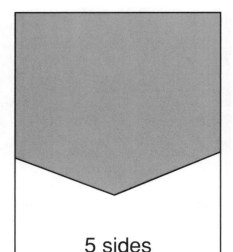

6 sides

6 angles

4 sides

4 angles

Opposite sides are of equal length.

5 sides

5 angles

For Every Learner™: Math • ©The Mailbox® Books • TEC61196 • Key p. 79

Note to the teacher: Use with "Shaping Up" on page 45.

Juggling Fun

Color by the code.
Then complete each sentence.

1. A triangle has ____ sides and
   ____ angles.

2. A circle has ____ sides and
   ____ angles.

3. A rectangle has ____ sides and
   ____ angles.

4. A square has ____ equal sides
   and ____ angles.

5. A trapezoid has ____ sides and
   ____ angles.

6. A pentagon has ____ sides and
   ____ angles.

7. A hexagon has ____ sides and
   ____ angles.

Color Code

triangle = yellow

circle = red

rectangle = green

square = orange

trapezoid = purple

pentagon = blue

hexagon = brown

For Every Learner™: *Math* • ©The Mailbox® Books • TEC61196 • Key p. 79

A Hungry Bear

1. Cut apart the cards.
2. Sort the cards into two sets as desired.
3. Glue each set to another sheet of paper.
4. Write a sentence or two above each set explaining how the shapes are sorted.

For Every Learner™: Math • ©The Mailbox® Books • TEC61196

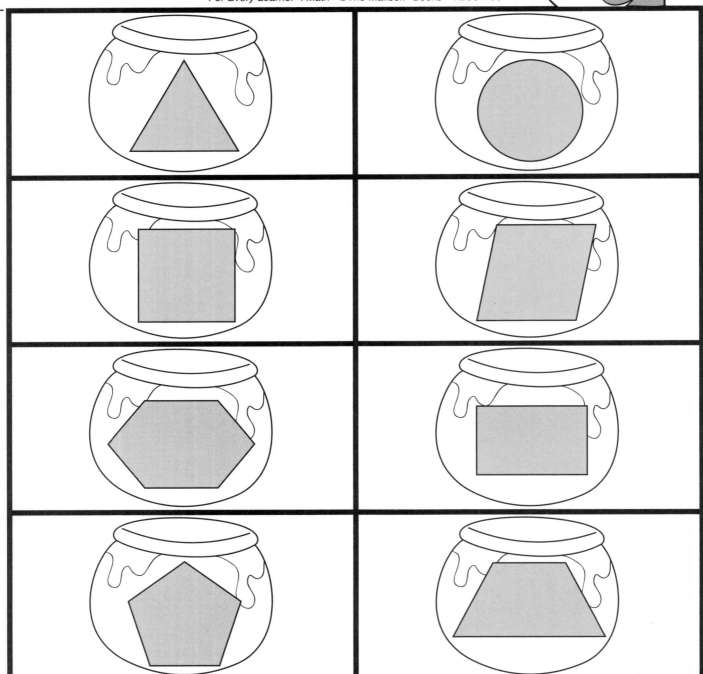

At the Art Gallery

(Pages 49 and 50)

1. Cut apart the cards.
2. Use the cards to write the name of the solid shape that matches each description on your other page.
3. Glue each card to the matching picture frame.

For Every Learner™: Math • ©The Mailbox® Books • TEC61196

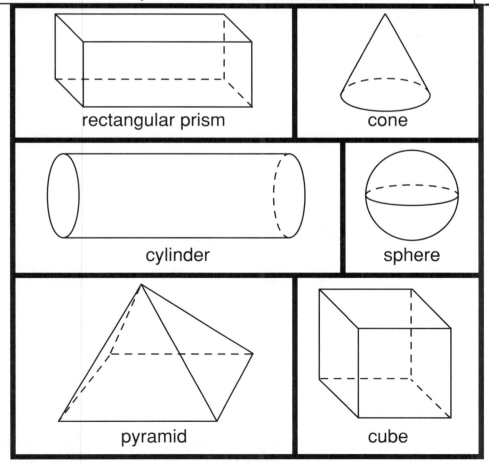

rectangular prism	cone
cylinder	sphere
pyramid	cube

At the Art Gallery

Glue here.

5 faces
8 edges
5 vertices

_____

Glue here.

6 equal faces
12 equal edges
8 vertices

_____

Glue here.

6 faces
12 edges
8 vertices

_____

Glue here.

0 faces
0 edges
0 vertices

_____

Glue here.

1 face
0 edges
0 vertices

_____

Glue here.

2 faces
0 edges
0 vertices

_____

For Every Learner™: Math • ©The Mailbox® Books • TEC61196 • Key p. 79

Note to the Teacher: Use with "At the Art Gallery" on page 49.

What Do You See?

Circle the name of each solid figure.

 sphere

cylinder

 pyramid

sphere

 cone

rectangular prism

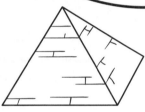 sphere

pyramid

 triangular prism

cube

 triangular prism

cylinder

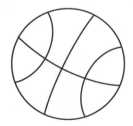 sphere

cone

 pyramid

rectangular prism

 cube

cylinder

 rectangular prism

cube

Catch a Wave!

1. Cut apart the cards.
2. Match each solid shape to its description.
3. Glue each set of cards to another sheet of paper.
4. Write the name of each solid shape above each set.

For Every Learner™: Math • ©The Mailbox® Books • TEC61196 • Key p. 79

I have zero faces. TEC61196	I have six faces. They are not all equal.	I have one face. It is a circle.
I have six faces. They are all squares.	I have two faces. My faces are circles.	I have five faces. Four of my faces are triangles.
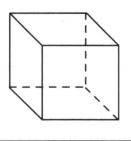	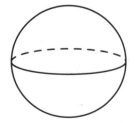	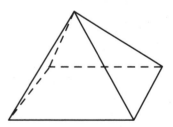
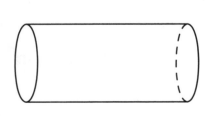	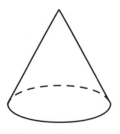	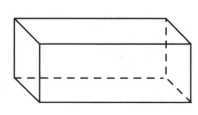

Clock Cutups

1. Cut apart the cards.
2. Match each time to a clock. Make
   a ●, ▼, or ■.
3. Glue each match to another sheet
   of paper.

For Every Learner™: *Math* • ©The Mailbox® Books • TEC61196 • Key p. 79

1:45	6:15	7:30
9:15	2:45	4:00
8:00	5:45	11:30

53

Time to Measure

Write the time shown on each clock.
Color the spice jar with the matching time.

A. _____

B. _____

C. _____

D. _____

Psssst! There are two extra spice jars.

E. _____

F. _____

10:15   9:45   11:15   3:30   6:00   8:30   1:15   2:00   4:45   12:15   5:30

7:45

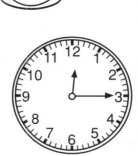

G. _____

H. _____

I. _____

J. _____

For Every Learner™: *Math* • ©The Mailbox® Books • TEC61196 • Key p. 79

A Busy Day

(Pages 55 and 56)

1. Write the time on each card.
2. Cut apart the cards.
3. Order the cards from the earliest time to the latest time.
4. On your other page, glue the cards in order.

_____ : _____ PM   _____ : _____ AM   _____ : _____ PM   _____ : _____ AM

_____ : _____ AM   _____ : _____ PM   _____ : _____ PM   _____ : _____ PM

_____ : _____ PM   _____ : _____ PM   _____ : _____ AM   _____ : _____ PM

56

A Busy Day

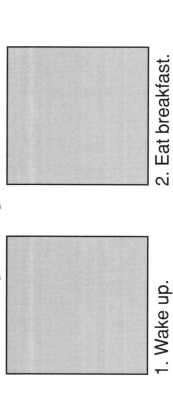

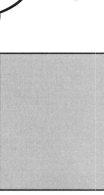

1. Wake up.

2. Eat breakfast.

3. Get dressed.

4. Go to school.

5. Eat lunch.

6. Come home.

7. Eat a snack.

8. Play outside.

9. Do homework.

10. Eat dinner.

11. Read a book.

12. Go to bed.

For Every Learner™: *Math* • ©The Mailbox® Books • TEC61196 • Key p. 79

Note to the teacher: Use with "A Busy Day" on page 55.

Shopping for Scents

(Pages 57 and 58)

1. Cut out the coin cards below.
2. On your other page, glue the coin cards in the boxes to make each amount shown.

For Every Learner™: *Math* • ©The Mailbox® Books • TEC61196

Shopping for Scents

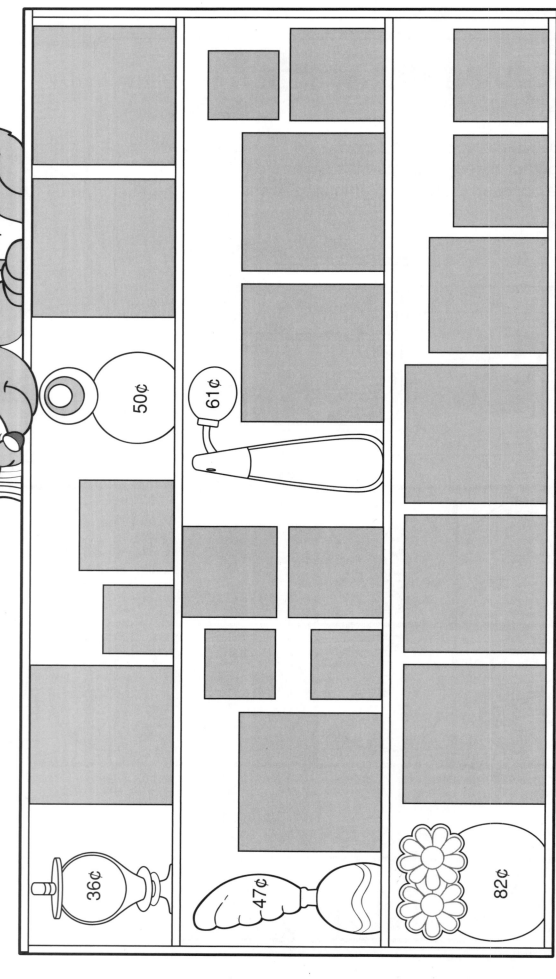

50¢

61¢

36¢

47¢

82¢

Note to the teacher: Use with "Shopping for Scents" on page 57.

Ready to Race!

Directions for two players:

1. Put your game markers on START.
2. In turn, roll a die and move your marker. Then count the coins on the space and say the amount.
3. If correct, leave your marker. If incorrect, move your marker back one space.
4. The first player to reach FINISH wins.

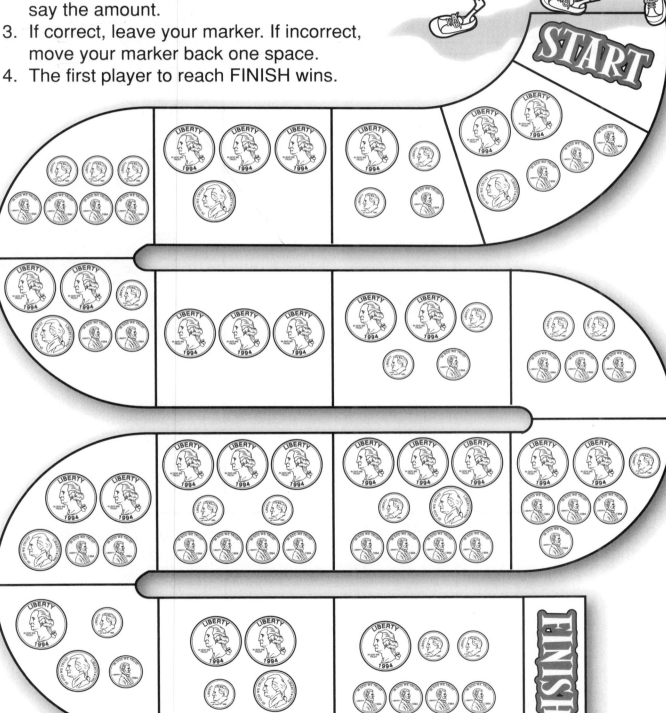

Saving Money

Use the coin code to make each coin amount.

Coin Code

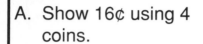 = quarter   Ⓓ = dime

Ⓝ = nickel   Ⓟ = penny

A. Show 16¢ using 4 coins.

B. Show 45¢ using 5 coins.

C. Show 37¢ using 7 coins.

D. Show 62¢ using 5 coins.

E. Show 59¢ using 10 coins.

F. Show 24¢ using 8 coins.

G. Show 51¢ using 7 coins.

H. Show 76¢ using 6 coins.

Plenty of Puppies

Cut apart the puppy cards.
Glue each card in the correct section of the Venn diagram.

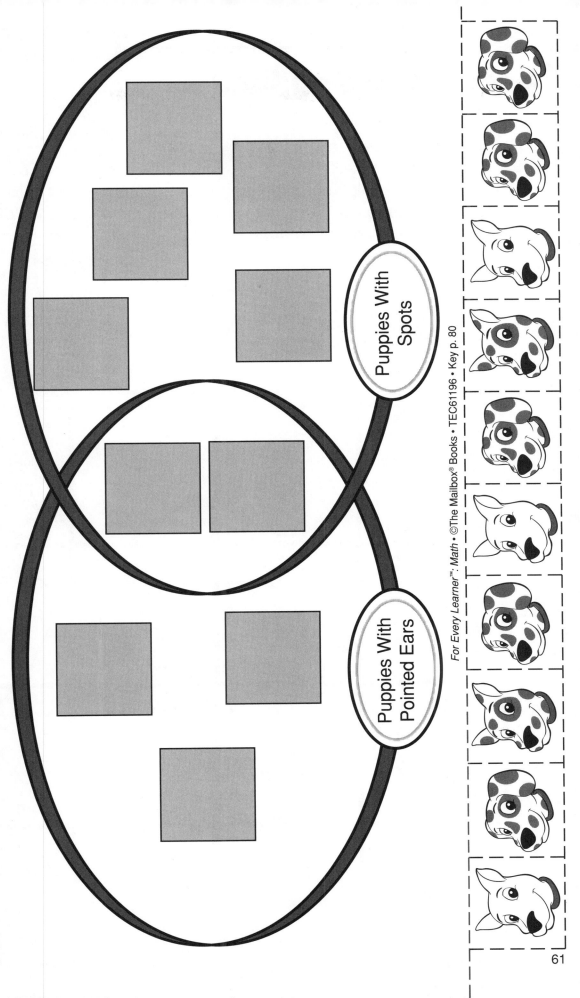

Puppies With
Spots

Puppies With
Pointed Ears

For Every Learner™: Math • ©The Mailbox® Books • TEC61196 • Key p. 80

Farm Fresh Produce

(Pages 62 and 63)

1. Cut apart the cards.
2. Sort the cards by vegetable.
3. Use the cards to help you complete the bar graph on your other page.
4. Use the completed graph to answer the questions on your other page.

corn   eggplant   carrots

For Every Learner™: Math • ©The Mailbox® Books • TEC61196

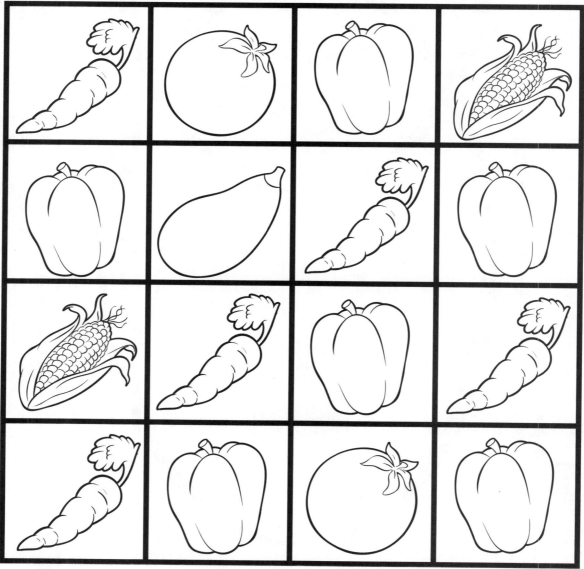

Farm Fresh Produce

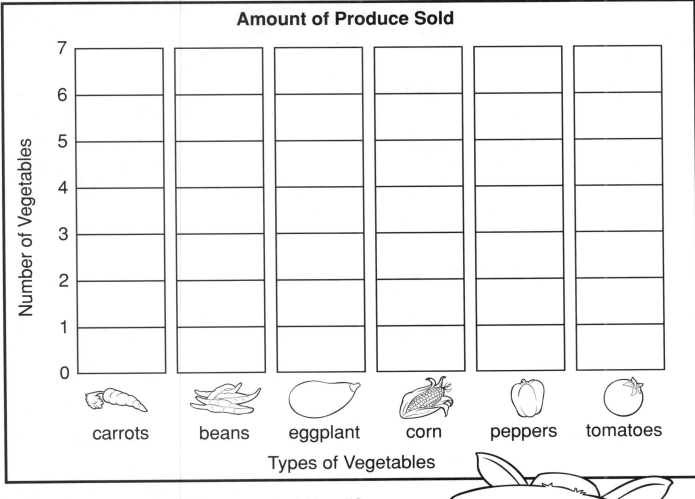

Amount of Produce Sold

Number of Vegetables

7
6
5
4
3
2
1
0

carrots   beans   eggplant   corn   peppers   tomatoes

Types of Vegetables

1. How many vegetables were sold in all?

   _____

2. How many fewer tomatoes than carrots were sold? _____

3. How many more peppers than carrots were sold? _____

4. If the farmer wanted to sell 7 ears of corn, how many more would he have had to sell?

   _____

5. Of which vegetable were the fewest sold?

   _____

For Every Learner™: Math • ©The Mailbox® Books • TEC61196 • Key p. 80

Note to the teacher: Use with "Farm Fresh Produce" on page 62.

63

What's the Weather?

Make a dot on the graph to show each day's temperature.
Then connect the dots to make a line graph.

Sun.	Mon.	Tues.	Wed.	Thurs.	Fri.	Sat.
12°F	25°F	18°F	24°F	29°F	33°F	27°F

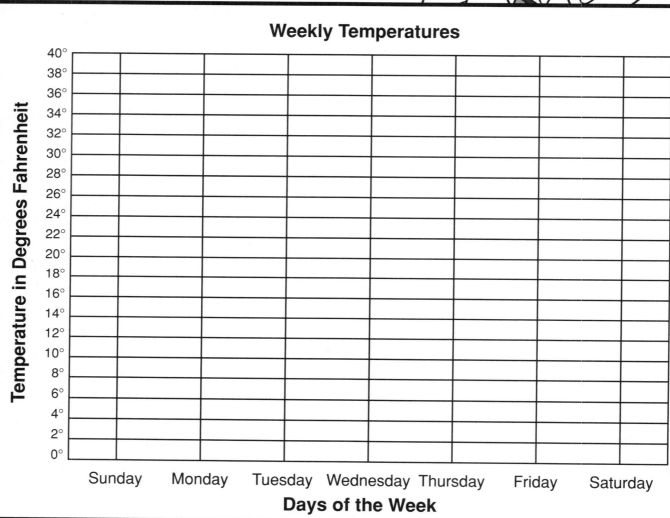

Weekly Temperatures

Temperature in Degrees Fahrenheit

40°
38°
36°
34°
32°
30°
28°
26°
24°
22°
20°
18°
16°
14°
12°
10°
8°
6°
4°
2°
0°

Sunday   Monday   Tuesday   Wednesday   Thursday   Friday   Saturday

Days of the Week

Write a summary of the data displayed in the line graph.

_____

_____

_____

_____

Taking a Trip

The pie chart shows how much room each type of item takes in Bear's suitcase. Circle the answer to each question.

1. Which items take more space?		sHoes	sockS
2. Which items take less space?		shirts	pants
3. Which items take more space?		hats	towels
4. Which items take the same amount of space as the shoes?	pants	hats
5. Which items take more space than the towels?		shirts	pants
6. Which items take the most space?		socks	shirts

Where is Bear going on vacation?
To find out, write the underlined letter in each answer you circled from above in order on the lines below.

Bear is going to ___ ___ ___ ___ ___ ___!

Mix and Match

Use the pictograph to help you answer each question.

= 2 shoes

Stella's Shoes

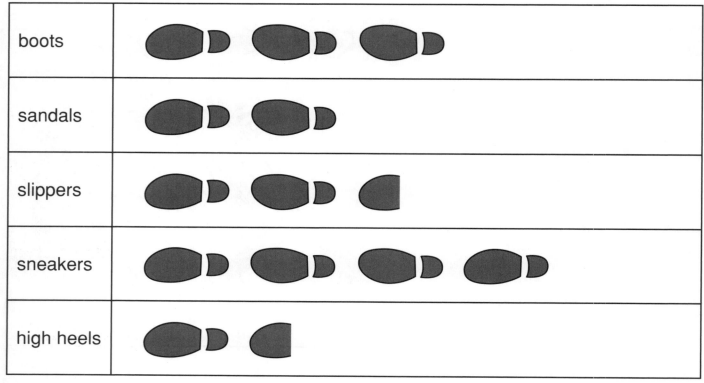

boots	
sandals	
slippers	
sneakers	
high heels	

1. Of which kind of shoes does Stella have the most? _____

   How many does she have? _____

2. Of which kind of shoes does Stella have the least? _____

   How many does she have? _____

3. How many boots and high heels does Stella have altogether? _____

4. How many more sneakers than slippers does Stella have? _____

5. How many fewer high heels than boots does Stella have? _____

   For Every Learner™: Math • ©The Mailbox® Books • TEC61196 • Key p. 80

Alphabet Soup

(Pages 67 and 68)

1. Cut apart the cards.
2. Read each card. Look at the graph on your other page. Sort the cards into two piles: true and false.
3. Write each letter in the correct bowl on your other page.

For Every Learner™: Math • ©The Mailbox® Books • TEC61196

B There are 6 *E*s in Owl's bowl.	**C** There are more *O*s than *E*s.	**D** There are 6 more *O*s than *U*s.
F Owl found fewer *E*s than any other vowel.	**G** In all, there are 10 *E*s and *U*s in the bowl.	**H** There are 6 *A*s in the bowl.
J There are more *E*s than *A*s.	**K** There are 10 *O*s in Owl's bowl.	**L** There are fewer *O*s than *I*s.
M There are 8 *E*s in Owl's bowl.	**N** There are more *O*s than any other vowel.	**P** There are 2 more *A*s than *E*s.
Q There are 4 *U*s in Owl's bowl.	**R** There are fewer *E*s than *U*s.	**S** There are 12 *I*s in Owl's bowl.
T There are more *I*s than any other vowel.	**V** There are 8 *O*s in Owl's bowl.	**W** Altogether, there are 14 *A*s and *E*s in Owl's bowl.
X Altogether, there are 12 *O*s and *U*s in the bowl.	**Y** There are 8 *A*s in Owl's bowl.	**Z** Owl found fewer *U*s than any other vowel.

Alphabet Soup

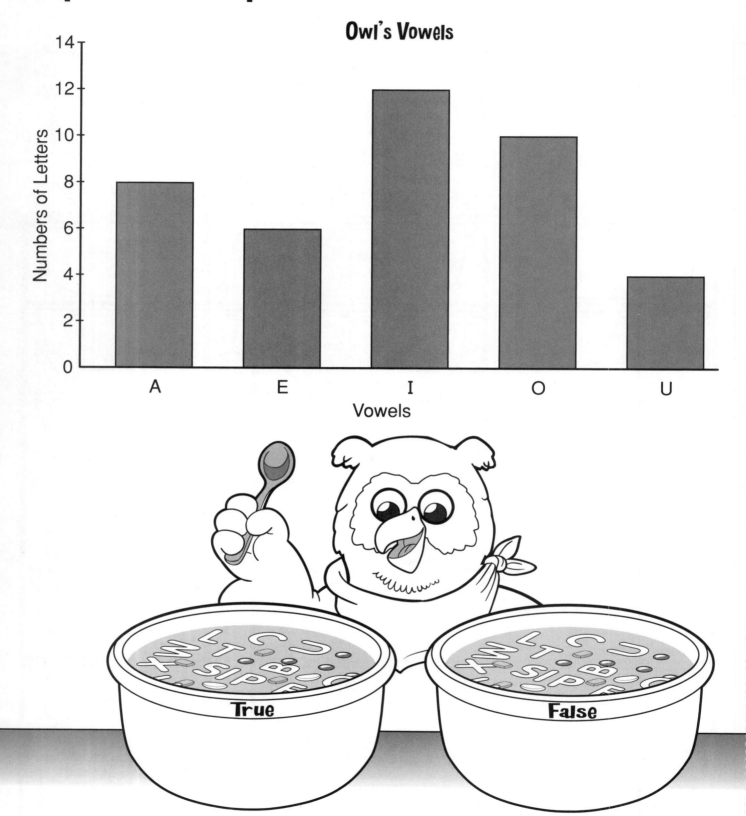

Owl's Vowels

For Every Learner™: Math • ©The Mailbox® Books • TEC61196 • Key p. 80

Name _____

Skipping Stones

Write the numbers to continue each pattern.

A. Count by ones.
1, 2, 3, 4, ____, ____, ____

B. Count by threes.
3, 6, 9, 12, ____, ____, ____

C. Count backward by twos.
14, 12, 10, 8, ____, ____, ____

D. Count by fives.
5, 10, 15, 20, ____, ____, ____

E. Count backward by ones.
23, 22, 21, 20, ____, ____, ____

F. Count by odd numbers.
1, 3, 5, 7, ____, ____, ____

G. Count backward by fours.
28, 24, 20, 16, ____, ____, ____

H. Count backward by tens.
80, 70, 60, 50, ____, ____, ____

Color the stone that matches the last number in each pattern.

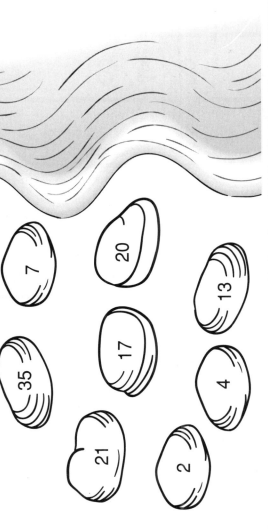

Follow the Rules!

(Pages 70 and 71)

1. Complete each pattern.
2. Cut apart the strips.
3. Glue each strip to the matching rule on your other page.

For Every Learner™: Math • ©The Mailbox® Books • TEC61196

1, 2, 4, 8, _____, _____, _____
4, 8, _____, 16, 20, _____, _____
35, _____, 25, 20, _____, 10, _____
1, 2, 2, 3, 4, 4, _____, _____, _____
3; 33; _____; 3,333; _____; _____
99, 88, _____, 66, _____, 44, _____
2, 6, 5, 9, 8, 12, _____, _____, _____
9, 7, 8, 9, _____, 8, _____, 7, _____

Name

Follow the Rules!

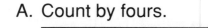

A. Count by fours.

B. Subtract 11.

C. Repeat 9, 7, 8.

D. Count by ones, writing the even numbers twice.

E. Using only the number 3, add a place value to each new number.

F. Add 4, subtract 1, repeat.

G. Double each number.

H. Count backward by fives.

For Every Learner™: Math • ©The Mailbox® Books • TEC61196 • Key p. 80

système

On the Lookout

1. Complete each pattern.
2. Cut apart the cards.
3. Glue each card to another sheet of paper.
4. Write below each card the rule for the pattern.

For Every Learner™: Math • ©The Mailbox® Books • TEC61196 • Key p. 80

50, 45, ____, 35, 30, ____, 20, 15

14, 24, 34, 44, ____, 64, 74, ____

1, 7, 13, ____, 25, ____, 37, 43

____, 36, 32, 28, 24, 20, ____, 12

90, 80, 70, ____, 50, 40, ____, 20

3, 4, ____, 3, 4, 5, ____, 4, 5

1, 3, 5, ____, ____, 11, 13, 15

____, 18, 21, 24, ____, 30, 33, 36

Boning Up!

1. Cut out the bone halves.
2. On another sheet of paper, glue each addition fact beside its related subtraction fact.

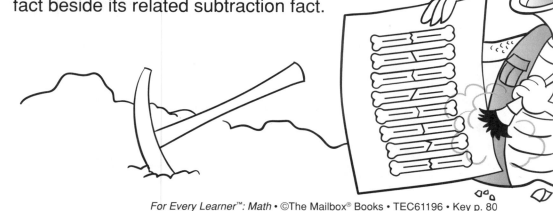

$4 + 7 = 11$

$5 + 7 = 12$

$11 - 7 = 4$

$3 + 5 = 8$

$7 + 8 = 15$

$16 - 7 = 9$

$9 + 7 = 16$

$8 - 5 = 3$

$13 - 9 = 4$

$8 + 6 = 14$

$10 - 7 = 3$

$15 - 8 = 7$

$3 + 7 = 10$

$12 - 7 = 5$

$4 + 9 = 13$

$14 - 6 = 8$

Out of This World

Draw a line to match each pair of symbols.
Use the related fact to find the missing number.

____ + 9 = 13		

____ + 9 = 13

7 + ____ = 16

____ + 6 = 12

____ + 5 = 7

8 + ____ = 15

10 – ____ = 2

17 – ____ = 8

11 – ____ = 3

15 – ____ = 9

14 – ____ = 7

____ + 7 = 13

12 – ____ = 4

15 – 8 = 7

14 – 7 = 7

13 – 9 = 4

12 – 4 = 8

17 – 8 = 9

16 – 7 = 9

7 – 5 = 2

11 – 3 = 8

13 – 7 = 6

10 – 2 = 8

12 – 6 = 6

15 – 9 = 6

Gems for Sale

(Pages 75 and 76)

1. Cut apart the cards below.
2. Use the numbers on each card to complete the number sentences by the matching gem on your other page.

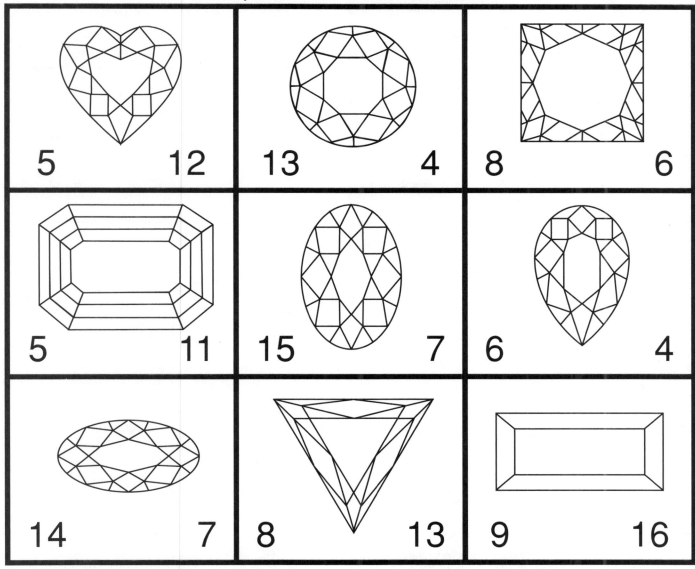

5 12	13 4	8 6
5 11	15 7	6 4
14 7	8 13	9 16

Gems for Sale

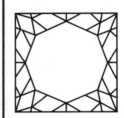 ____ + ____ = 14

14 − ____ = ____

 ____ + 5 = ____

____ − ____ = 5

 ____ + ____ = 10

10 − ____ = ____

 9 + ____ = ____

____ − ____ = 9

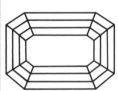 6 + ____ = ____

____ − ____ = 6

 ____ + 7 = ____

____ − 7 = ____

 7 + ____ = ____

____ − 7 = ____

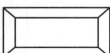 ____ + 7 = ____

____ − ____ = 7

 ____ + 8 = ____

____ − ____ = 8

For Every Learner™: Math • ©The Mailbox® Books • TEC61196 • Key p. 80

Answer Keys

Page 5
A. 56 B. 73 C. 43 D. 95
E. 59 F. 84 G. 97 H. 49
I. 66 J. 75 K. 77 L. 88

Page 7
A. 67 B. 48 C. 89 D. 84 E. 25
F. 76 G. 47 H. 98 I. 56 J. 79
K. 98 L. 77

Page 8
Order may vary.

123 + 872 995	123 + 435 558	123 + 260 383
123 + 446 569	123 + 631 754	214 + 582 796
214 + 303 517	214 + 255 469	214 + 611 825
214 + 364 578		

Page 9

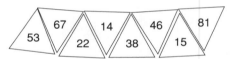
53 67 22 14 38 46 15 81

Page 10
A. 45 B. 23 C. 50 D. 52
E. 63 F. 21 G. 44 H. 43
I. 44 J. 23
Problem E should be colored.

Page 13
A. 80 B. 51 C. 46 E. 68
F. 67 H. 82 M. 93 S. 73

<u>THEY BAKE FROM SCRATCH</u>!

Page 15
A. 53 B. 83 C. 81
D. 93 E. 40 F. 85
G. 91 H. 43
I. 62 J. 91

Page 16

Correct   Incorrect

Correct	Incorrect
136 + 382 = 518	250 + 193 = 343
312 + 197 = 509	413 + 207 = 610
227 + 198 = 425	318 + 264 = 583
234 + 396 = 630	175 + 186 = 260
215 + 127 = 342	184 + 309 = 483
352 + 184 = 536	271 + 456 = 637

Page 17

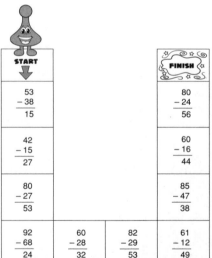

START → FINISH

53 − 38 = 15
42 − 15 = 27
80 − 27 = 53
92 − 68 = 24   60 − 28 = 32   82 − 29 = 53   61 − 12 = 49

80 − 24 = 56
60 − 16 = 44
85 − 47 = 38

Page 18
A. 26
B. 13
C. 56
D. 8
E. 58
F. 16
G. 29
H. 9
I. 17
J. 16
K. 19
L. 25

Page 20
Order of problems in each row will vary.

607 − 561 46	607 − 254 353	561 − 254 307
739 − 456 283	739 − 247 492	456 − 247 209
962 − 571 391	962 − 128 834	571 − 128 443
806 − 740 66	806 − 321 485	740 − 321 419
658 − 364 294	658 − 129 529	364 − 129 235

Page 21

146
305
613
490
536
974
721
857
1,000
389
408
760

Page 23
A. 145   1 hundred 4 tens 5 ones
B. 417   4 hundreds 1 ten 7 ones
C. 433   4 hundreds 3 tens 3 ones
D. 259   2 hundreds 5 tens 9 ones
E. 321   3 hundreds 2 tens 1 one
F. 94   9 tens 4 ones
G. 460   4 hundreds 6 tens 0 ones
H. 162   1 hundred 6 tens 2 ones
I. 1,000 1 thousand 0 hundreds 0 tens 0 ones
J. 340   3 hundreds 4 tens 0 ones
K. 502   5 hundreds 0 tens 2 ones
L. 712   7 hundreds 1 ten 2 ones

Page 24

1<u>2</u>6 — 100 G	2<u>3</u>6 — 30 R	<u>1</u>63 — 100 G
7<u>0</u>4 — 0 R	40<u>7</u> — 7 B	79<u>5</u> — 5 B
<u>8</u>61 — 800 G	<u>3</u>67 — 300 G	69<u>2</u> — 2 B
<u>2</u>72 — 200 G	<u>1</u>,000 — 1,000 Y	<u>9</u>58 — 900 G
53<u>0</u> — 0 B	3<u>4</u>9 — 40 R	51<u>8</u> — 8 B

Answers will vary.

Page 25

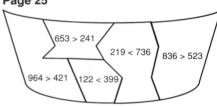

653 > 241
219 < 736
836 > 523
964 > 421
122 < 399

Page 28

A. <   K. <
B. >   L. <
C. <   M. <
D. >   N. =
E. =   O. >
F. >
G. <
H. =
I. >
J. <

No.
Answers will vary.

Page 30

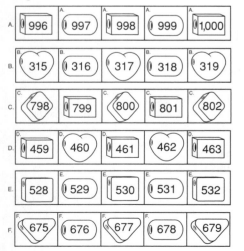

A. 996 997 998 999 1,000
B. 315 316 317 318 319
C. 798 799 800 801 802
D. 459 460 461 462 463
E. 528 529 530 531 532
F. 675 676 677 678 679

Page 31

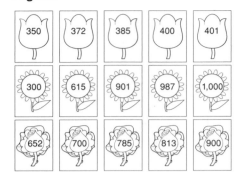

350 372 385 400 401
300 615 901 987 1,000
652 700 785 813 900

Page 32

136, 163, 316, 361, 613, 631
852, 825, 582, 528, 285, 258
459, 495, 549, 594, 945, 954
871, 817, 781, 718, 187, 178
356, 365, 536, 563, 635, 653
1,000, 954, 871, 852, 653, 631

Page 34

A. 7 + 8 = 15   B. 8 − 2 = 6
C. 7 + 6 = 13   D. 8 − 7 = 1
E. 15 − 6 = 9   F. 6 + 2 = 8

Page 35

A.
```
  43
+ 36
  79
```
B.
```
  78
− 26
  52
```
C.
```
  97
− 42
  55
```
D.
```
  47
+ 38
  85
```
E.
```
  64
− 21
  43
```
F.
```
  24
+ 24
  48
```

Page 36

Order may vary.

Addition

A.
```
  126
+  49
  175
```
D.
```
  48
+ 17
  65
```
F.
```
  74
+ 65
  139
```

Subtraction

B.
```
  83
− 35
  48
```
C.
```
  126
−  52
   74
```
E.
```
  83
− 65
  18
```

Page 37

Order may vary.

Less than $5.00
```
$ 4 . 78
− 1 . 24
$ 3 . 54
```
```
$ 4 . 63
− 2 . 41
$ 2 . 22
```
```
$ 7 . 96
− 3 . 24
$ 4 . 72
```

More than $5.00
```
$ 3 . 14
+ 4 . 23
$ 7 . 37
```
```
$ 1 . 46
+ 4 . 42
$ 5 . 88
```
```
$ 4 . 12
+ 5 . 81
$ 9 . 93
```

Page 39

1. $7.97
2. $1.14
3. $2.44
4. $4.81
5. $3.65
6. $4.32

Page 40

1.
```
  $6.85
−   .72
  $6.13
```
2.
```
  $6.13
+  1.84
  $7.97
```
3.
```
  $7.97
−  2.11
  $5.86
```
4.
```
  $5.86
−   .75
  $5.11
```
5.
```
  $5.11
+  2.75
  $7.86
```
6.
```
  $7.86
−  6.85
  $1.01
```

Page 41

Order may vary.

Less than ½

 $\frac{1}{6}$

 $\frac{1}{5}$

 $\frac{1}{3}$

 $\frac{2}{5}$

 $\frac{2}{8}$

 $\frac{1}{4}$

More than ½

 $\frac{4}{6}$

 $\frac{3}{4}$

 $\frac{2}{3}$

 $\frac{3}{5}$

 $\frac{5}{6}$

 $\frac{6}{8}$

Page 44

A. $\frac{1}{3}$ < $\frac{2}{4}$		B. $\frac{5}{6}$ > $\frac{1}{4}$	
C. $\frac{2}{5}$ < $\frac{2}{3}$		D. $\frac{3}{6}$ = $\frac{1}{2}$	
E. $\frac{4}{8}$ = $\frac{1}{2}$		F. $\frac{7}{8}$ > $\frac{3}{4}$	
G. $\frac{3}{4}$ > $\frac{2}{3}$		H. $\frac{1}{2}$ < $\frac{4}{5}$	
I. $\frac{1}{8}$ < $\frac{1}{4}$		J. $\frac{2}{3}$ > $\frac{3}{6}$	

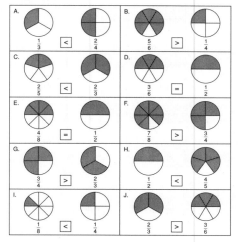

Page 46

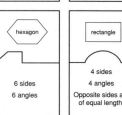 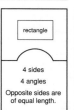

triangle — 3 sides, 3 angles

circle — 0 sides, 0 angles

square — 4 sides, 4 angles, All sides are of equal length.

hexagon — 6 sides, 6 angles

rectangle — 4 sides, 4 angles, Opposite sides are of equal length.

pentagon — 5 sides, 5 angles

Page 47

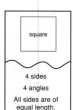 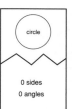 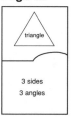 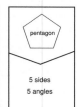

1. A triangle had **3** sides and **3** angles.
2. A circle has **0** sides and **0** angles.
3. A rectangle has **4** sides and **4** angles.
4. A square has **4** equal sides and **4** angles.
5. A trapezoid has **4** sides and **4** angles.
6. A pentagon has **5** sides and **5** angles.
7. A hexagon has **6** sides and **6** angles.

Page 50

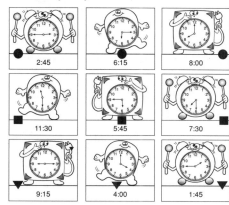

pyramid, cube, rectangular prism, sphere, cone, cylinder

Page 51

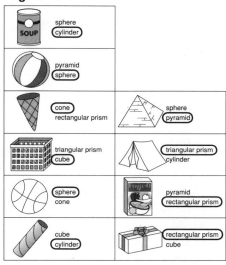

SOUP	sphere / (cylinder)		
beach ball	pyramid / (sphere)		
cone	(cone) rectangular prism	pyramid	sphere / (pyramid)
building	triangular prism / (cube)	tent	(triangular prism) cylinder
basketball	(sphere) cone	book	pyramid / (rectangular prism)
cylinder	cube / (cylinder)	gift	(rectangular prism) cube

Page 52

Order may vary.

 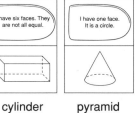

sphere — I have zero faces.

rectangular prism — I have six faces. They are not all equal.

cone — I have one face. It is a circle.

cube — I have six faces. They are all squares.

cylinder — I have two faces. My faces are circles.

pyramid — I have five faces. Four of my faces are triangles.

Page 53

Order may vary.

 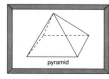 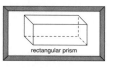 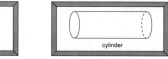

2:45	6:15	8:00
11:30	5:45	7:30
9:15	4:00	1:45

Page 54

A. 8:30
B. 11:15
C. 6:00
D. 9:45
E. 4:45
F. 1:15
G. 3:30
H. 2:00
I. 7:45
J. 12:15

Page 56

7:00 AM	7:15 AM	7:30 AM	8:00 AM
1. Wake up.	2. Eat breakfast.	3. Get dressed.	4. Go to school.
12:15 PM	3:30 PM	3:45 PM	4:15 PM
5. Eat lunch.	6. Come home.	7. Eat a snack.	8. Play outside.
5:00 PM	6:15 PM	6:45 PM	8:30 PM
9. Do homework.	10. Eat dinner.	11. Read a book.	12. Go to bed.

Page 58

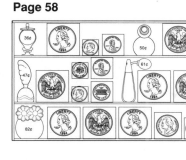 

Page 59

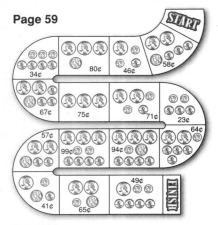

Page 60

A. Ⓝ Ⓝ Ⓝ Ⓟ

B. Ⓓ Ⓓ Ⓓ Ⓓ Ⓝ or Ⓠ Ⓝ Ⓝ Ⓝ Ⓝ

C. Ⓓ Ⓓ Ⓝ Ⓝ Ⓝ Ⓟ Ⓟ

D. Ⓠ Ⓠ Ⓓ Ⓟ Ⓟ

E. Ⓓ Ⓓ Ⓓ Ⓓ Ⓝ Ⓟ Ⓟ Ⓟ Ⓟ

F. Ⓝ Ⓝ Ⓝ Ⓝ Ⓟ Ⓟ Ⓟ Ⓟ

G. Ⓓ Ⓓ Ⓓ Ⓓ Ⓝ Ⓝ Ⓟ

H. Ⓠ Ⓠ Ⓓ Ⓝ Ⓟ

Page 61

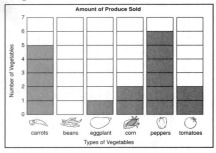

Page 63

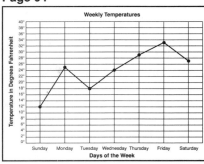

1. 16
2. 3
3. 1
4. 5
5. beans

Page 64

Answers will vary.

Page 65

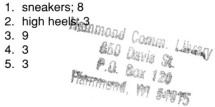

Bear is going to Hawaii!

Page 66

1. sneakers; 8
2. high heels; 3
3. 9
4. 3
5. 3

Page 68

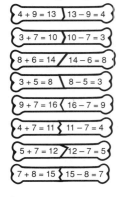

Page 69

A. 1, 2, 3, 4, _5_, _6_, _7_

B. 3, 6, 9, 12, _15_, _18_, _21_

C. 14, 12, 10, 8, _6_, _4_, _2_

D. 5, 10, 15, 20, _25_, _30_, _35_

E. 23, 22, 21, 20, _19_, _18_, _17_

F. 1, 3, 5, 7, _9_, _11_, _13_

G. 28, 24, 20, 16, _12_, _8_, _4_

H. 80, 70, 60, 50, _40_, _30_, _20_

Page 71

A. Count by fours.

4, 8, _12_, 16, 20, _24_, _28_

B. Subtract 11.

99, 88, _77_, 66, _55_, 44, _33_

C. Repeat 9, 7, 8.

9, 7, 8, 9, _7_, 8, _9_, 7, _8_

D. Count by ones, writing the even numbers twice.

1, 2, 2, 3, 4, 4, _5_, _6_, _6_

E. Using only the number 3, add a place value to each new number.

3; 33; _333_; 3,333; _33,333_; _333,333_

F. Add 4, subtract 1, repeat.

2, 6, 5, 9, 8, 12, _11_, _15_, _14_

G. Double each number.

1, 2, 4, 8, _16_, _32_, _64_

H. Count backward by fives.

35, _30_, 25, 20, _15_, 10, _5_

Page 65 (items)

1. Which items take more space? — sHoes / sockS
2. Which items take less space? — shirts / pants
3. Which items take more space? — hats / towels
4. Which items take the same amount of space as the shoes? — pants / hats
5. Which items take more space than the towels? — shirts / pants
6. Which items take the most space? — socks / shirts

Page 72

Order may vary.

_15_, 18, 21, 24, _27_, 30, 33, 36
Add 3.

1, 7, 13, _19_, 25, _31_, 37, 43
Add 6.

50, 45, _40_, 35, 30, _25_, 20, 15
Count backward by fives.

90, 80, 70, _60_, 50, 40, _30_, 20
Count backward by tens.

_40_, 36, 32, 28, 24, 20, _16_, 12
Subtract 4.

3, 4, _5_, 3, 4, 5, _3_, 4, 5
Repeat 3, 4, 5.

14, 24, 34, 44, _54_, 64, 74, _84_
Add 10.

1, 3, 5, _7_, 9, _11_, 13, 15
Add 2.

Page 73

Order may vary.

4 + 9 = 13 / 13 − 9 = 4

3 + 7 = 10 / 10 − 7 = 3

8 + 6 = 14 / 14 − 6 = 8

3 + 5 = 8 / 8 − 5 = 3

9 + 7 = 16 / 16 − 7 = 9

4 + 7 = 11 / 11 − 7 = 4

5 + 7 = 12 / 12 − 7 = 5

7 + 8 = 15 / 15 − 8 = 7

Page 74

_4_ + 9 = 13

7 + _9_ = 16

_6_ + 6 = 12

_2_ + 5 = 7

8 + _7_ = 15

10 − _8_ = 2

17 − _9_ = 8

11 − _8_ = 3

15 − _6_ = 9

14 − _7_ = 7

_6_ + 7 = 13

12 − _8_ = 4

15 − 8 = 7

14 − 7 = 7

13 − 9 = 4

12 − 4 = 8

17 − 8 = 9

16 − 7 = 9

7 − 5 = 2

11 − 3 = 8

13 − 7 = 6

10 − 2 = 8

12 − 6 = 6

15 − 9 = 6

Page 76

Order of numbers may vary.

_6_ + _8_ = 14
14 − _6_ = _8_

_8_ + 5 = 13
13 − _8_ = 5

4 + _6_ = 10
10 − _4_ = 6

9 + _4_ = 13
13 − _4_ = 9

6 + _5_ = 11
11 − _5_ = 6

_7_ + 7 = 14
14 − 7 = _7_

7 + _5_ = 12
12 − _7_ = 5

_9_ + 7 = 16
16 − _9_ = 7

_7_ + 8 = 15
15 − _7_ = 8